HR HEGNAUER

PORTABLE PRESS AT YO-YO LABS

NEW YORK

ISBN: 978-0-615-23100-6

Original cover art by Brenda Iijima:
"button down, biome, inspired by HR's youth"
Back cover image: Robert & Raymond Hook,
the author's grandfather and his brother, circa 1929.
Design & typesetting by HR Hegnauer.

This book was made possible with funds by the New York State Council on the
Arts, The Council of Literary Magazines and Presses, and individual donors.

Selections of this manuscript were previously published in *Bombay Gin*
and *Troubling the Line: Trans and Genderqueer Poetry and Poetics.* An early draft
was published in 2011 as a chapbook by Portable Press at Yo-Yo Labs.

Distributed by Small Press Distribution
1341 Seventh Street
Berkeley, California 94710
spdbooks.org

PORTABLE PRESS AT YO-YO LABS
Brooklyn, New York
www.yoyolabs.com

For my mother
& for her mother

and no whiteness (lost) is so white as the memory
of whiteness   .

WILLIAM CARLOS WILLIAMS

Don't miss anything.

The date was twelve-twenty, twenty-ten, and this was exactly what Mrs. Alice said to me. She even grabbed my hand and repeated it. I thought this was pretty fancy of her.

Of course, I told her, *I wouldn't.*

When I was still a little girl, Sir once jokingly said to me, *call me Sir.* And so I mostly called him Sir.

Mrs. Alice and Sir had each their own separate bathrooms, and inside of Sir's — which was the only one I used — was a special set of wooden brushes. There were three that hung from each their own separate hook with a little round mirror in the middle. Of course I knew these were Sir's special wooden brushes, and so when I'd brush their shepherd, I mostly liked to use the one on the left because it seemed to fit her the best. I don't think that Sir ever knew this, or if he did, I didn't know that he knew. Of if I did, I certainly don't remember this. And this is the way I like to hold this thought: with the subtleties of who knew what and when they knew it.

Every time we walk down this hallway, I hope that the lady with the gnarly teeth hasn't taken down the florescent-lit cross that hangs on her door. Not that I'm all that partial to florescent crosses, but I do know that Mrs. Alice knows that this is where you turn right. And if this lady ever changes, then how will Mrs. Alice know where to turn right?

Mrs. Alice and I have walked down this hallway a number of times now: before and after lunch, and before and after dinner, and during just about anytime that isn't exactly before or after any particular meal.

I am twenty-six-years-old, and — for the first time in my life — I have memories of myself as an adult. They vary in their lucidness, of course, but I can say that I have been an adult for a few years now, and I can remember what it is like to be one. My mother is exactly thirty years older than me, and Mrs. Alice is thirty years older than she, and I know I am not the only one between my mother and I who worries about the potentiality of dementia as being hereditary.

Mrs. Alice met Sir in high school. That was seventy years ago now. I don't really know how long seventy years is. I can only imagine most of twenty-six. How long is seventy?

I used to match my crew socks to Sir's: pulled up around our shins until a tan line so distinct would form that people thought we were painted ash white from the shins down when we'd walk around bare.

This is the part when Mrs. Alice would lean over the back of the couch and look out the front picture window with her camera to capture our matching gym-sock-covered shins. Sir would say, *walk steady now*, and I would say, *you know Hannah means graceful*, and Sir would say, *yeah, but you're always spelling that backwards*. This is how we'd walk down the driveway in the morning time. And when we'd return at noon, the pictures would be ready — printed in doubles, always.

We'd go along the marsh where Sir would tell me about the time he saw some guy dump an alligator into this exact spot because it got too big to live in his bathtub. I knew this was true, and so I'd look for it. And I'd think of the birds and the deer that lived in this field that didn't yet know about their alligator neighbor, but of course they'd know soon enough.

This was how we usually moved around this bay. Like a spliced thing trying to rivet its selves back together again, but not really knowing what this might actually look like anymore.

It was on one of our morning walks that Sir first told me about the ship. About how we could go there if I wanted to work. Of course I did, and so we did. And I got to wash the deck more than once. And then I got to sit in the grey metal chair that's connected to the big gun on the front of the deck, and I'd shoot. This was the good part; to sit in the gun-chair with my crew socks pulled up and shoot. Bullets and missiles and bombs and anything I could think of. This was how things operated on the ship. This was the deck washing prize.

This was before I was given a dolphin-shaped squirt gun as a party favor at my friend's birthday. Of course I knew that toy guns were not allowed, but I figured this would be an exception, seeing as how it was shaped like a dolphin. This was before I was told to get rid of it.

I buried the dolphin in the back of the garden — right between my goldfish, Alfred, and my rabbit, Sarah-The-Boy. The goldfish was named after the character in Guess Who who had orange hair because he looked just like him — having orange gills. The rabbit was named Sarah because I liked that name; then we found out that she was a he, but he liked his name, and so we kept it. Turned out he liked his full name even more — Sarah-The-Boy, and so we called him this, and this was never strange. The dolphin was buried nameless.

I learned about war for the first time in the first grade. We had just started fighting in the Persian Gulf. Mrs. Thom said that we wouldn't hear any bombs, but that they were real, and they were dangerous — more dangerous than anything we'd ever hope to know. I remember her telling me that we had never lost a war before, and that this was something to be proud of. When I walked home from school that day, Matt told me that not only had we never lost, but that we had never actually been to war until now. I told Sir that we had never been to war before, and now we're in the Gulf, but don't be afraid because we won't actually hear any bombs. I told him like I was an expert on the politics of war. He said, *then what the hell was I doing in 1944?* I said, *I don't know. Maybe it was only a battle and not actually a war.* Sir looked at me. I remember this look for sure like he's looking at me right now.

This was the same year that Sir came with my class to the zoo. Somehow I got him to volunteer to be a chaperone, which meant being in charge of twelve small children. By 9:00 a.m., he had already bought us each a cotton candy and a Slurpee, which turned our mouths blue and purple within seconds. After minutes, we were chasing one another atop the roof of the nocturnal house. I saw Mrs. Thom squinting in our direction from across the field, and she began to walk towards us with a real purpose. We jumped from the roof and grabbed Sir's hand, pulling him into the wooded area. We hid our tiny sugared bodies behind trees and under benches. Sir sat and waited for Mrs. Thom at the picnic table. Their voices sounded like the adults on the Muppets. I licked the sugar from between my fingers. We compared who had the bluest teeth. I became popular that week for bringing the best chaperone.

Mrs. Alice and I have been walking the hallways again. We like to look for the cat, but the cat went to a new home several months ago now, and I don't keep telling her this. We'll walk along one hallway, sit in the chair next to the stone statue of a cat, and she'll pretend it's real. We'll walk on. She'll call out, *Kitty, kitty, come here.* Mrs. Alice is always a bit sad when we can't find the cat, but as with everything, that's a fleeting feeling. This is a game of walking and forgetting. Walking and forgetting. We'll walk along a little further. She'll call out. I'll call out. Am I being exploitive? Perhaps so. When I look at Mrs. Alice, she'll smile at me. She knows we are looking for something — a lost something — but she can't remember what the thing is anymore. We'll rest again by the stone cat. This is an adventure without the mind.

Sir called late last weekend, around 10:30 or so. He said he couldn't get Mrs. Alice up out of her chair and into bed. I said, *What do you mean? ... Just come over.* And so we went. There was a puddle, and then I knew what Sir meant, too. I said, *Mrs. Alice, it's time to get up out of this chair ... I know,* she said, *I know. But I can't because, well, there's a puddle.* My mother held her forearm with her right hand and pushed against her lower back with her left, and she heaved her forward. I put the puddle in the garbage. I do not know how long Mrs. Alice had been sitting in her chair at the dining room table, and I do not like to think about how long or why either. Perhaps six hours or perhaps a few more really. It was as if she had all together forgotten she had a body anymore.

And then there was the embarrassment of remembering, *yes, I do have a body.*

I read somewhere that it's impossible to tell if dementia is hereditary or not because it is too common in elderly people.

When I was in the seventh grade, a motivational speaker came to my algebra class. He said he used to hate his life, and he'd begin each day by waking up and smoking a bowl. I thought about how big a cereal bowl is. He said that one morning he came to realize that to love someone means that you only want the greatest good for them. That's all that he said: *the greatest good*. I think this is pretty accurate. I had no idea what was in his cereal bowl.

Sir told me to pound back down each nail. I asked if we could replace the nails with screws instead, but he said that'd be too expensive, so *pound down the nails*. It was during times like this when Sir liked to call me Lackey, but I didn't know what that meant. He told me that it meant it was like I was his associate. It was 106 degrees outside on the deck, and even though I was twelve now and fairly nimble, I was exhausted from the beginning. Sir and I used to call this the pounding project, and I knew it well. Mrs. Alice said that I could have a root beer and brush the shepherd later, so I kept pounding.

That was exactly when the phone rang twice, and then Sir shut the bedroom door. When the door opened, I was waiting, *Who was that?* ... *Well, that was the President, of course.* That's what Sir always said, and I wanted to believe him, and so I did. And when I'd say this to Sunny across the street, he believed this, too. That's what made it true: two people believed it, and we said, *Yes, yes. The President was on the line.*

Someone said you had to be fifteen to start driving, but Sir said that thirteen was a good age, and I agreed. I walked down the block to the DMV to get my license, and the woman told me to go home. I said to her, *But I have straight A's, and I already know how to drive.* She said, *You need to leave now, or I'll call your mother.* I walked home. I walked back two years later, and they took my picture at the counter and handed me a card. This made it official.

I didn't tell them that I'd been driving for two years now — ever since that awful accident that Sir and Mrs. Alice and I witnessed along the backside of the armory outside of Oakland. That was the moment when all the wheels turned, and I became their driver. We watched a man flip his stolen car and drag his face along the freeway guardrail, through the windshield, across the shoulder, and towards the woods. Sir called to the man's upside down body, *Sir, sir can you hear me?! ... Dude, help me out of here!* He kept yelling this at us. *Dude, pull me out!* Then an ambulance came. A fire truck came. The police came, and then another fire truck came, and they all kept saying, *he's so methed-out. This guy's methed-out.* One uniformed-man came up to me, and said, *The only reason why this man is still alive is because he's so methed-out. Let this be a lesson to you.* I didn't know what this meant: methed-out. I looked at the man's badge and nodded. *Yes, I understand.* I thought to myself, *Remember this. This must be a safe place — this methed-out place.*

A few years later, the biggest meth lab West of the Mississippi blew up across the street from my high school. All the men with badges came again. We were sent home early — all of us kids — and we were told to think about what we've all just witnessed. The day turned into a project on visibility. All I could think about was that upside-down man along the freeway from a few years back, and how all he wanted was to get out. I heard him calling to me again, *Pull me out of here!* I heard him calling to Sir again, *Dude, pull me out of here!* I walked home from school. The next morning, I read in the paper that my county was the meth capital of the West.

Is this a project about remembering what losing your memory means? Yes. I think it is. One second. Now this second. Now this second, too. This is how the brain works in these moments: like a stutter, like a healthy stutter.

My mother and I just left Mrs. Alice. We pulled out onto the road and made the turns like we have a million times before. Right, left, right, left. We were quiet in our naturally quiet way. Let's see where the car takes us. We entered the exit ramp. I pulled at the wheel, *Not here! There! Go over there!* There were lights flashing. The man with the badge had the voice of a tape player, and all of his language seemed to exist as a result of a pull-cord along his back, *License and registration, Ma'am.* But for some reason, this simple request seemed completely unreasonable, or perhaps more accurately, it was too reasonable for a day that lacked all reason. *Ma'am, that's not the right paper. No, Ma'am, this one's expired. No, Ma'am, this one's expired, too. No, Ma'am, this is a ferry receipt. No, Ma'am, this is a disabled parking permit. No, Ma'am, this is a take-out menu . . . Well, what do you want then? Just tell me what you want!* By this point, my mother had nearly handed him the entire contents of the glove compartment. He looked at our pile and said, *Ma'am,* then tipped his hat and left.

This was not the first time I had entered the exit as a passenger. The first time was with Sir. He claimed the oncoming semi-truck was going the wrong direction. No men with badges came that day, but we pulled over anyway.

The other day I picked up Sir from the airport, and it was an ordeal, to say the least. I needed to meet him at the gate, not just at baggage claim. I stood at the special needs desk for what felt like eternity. I said, *he's 85-years-old. He needs assistance.* They said, *this should have been requested from the beginning.* I said, *it was.* Finally they let me pass in. I walked all of the twenty feet to the gate to meet Sir. They wouldn't let Danielle come with me. *Only one of you!* They kept saying this to me over the counter, *only one!* I felt like they were suspecting me for plotting something awful. And then when Sir finally got off the flight, we walked so slowly because naturally he was a bit tired, and the security guards kept looking at us, and I wanted to yell at them, *Where is your humanity?!* But I didn't because I don't think that Sir realized that we were being watched. We got his bag. We walked towards the car. Along the way, Sir nearly fell off the curb's edge. I pretended this was no big deal, and gently held his arm along his elbow.

My mother doesn't like to be called ma'am because it makes her feel old. My father doesn't like to be called sir because that just sounds strange. I like when people call me ma'am because it gives me hope that genders might be fluid. It becomes a special occasion for me, and I celebrate it by marking it on my calendar. But more often I'm called sir, and if I'm feeling extra confident, I like to respond, *I am not a sir!* I said this to an airport security officer in Denver when I was on my way to Sir's funeral, and I got patted down twice: first by a man and then by a woman. I thought about suing them.

I avoid public restrooms as a general rule. But when that's not possible — like in an extra-inning game — I take off my cap, walk in on a mission, and I don't make eye contact. I hate seeing when people double-check the icon on the door. That's why I like talking to telemarketers on the phone: they always call me ma'am.

Sir said to take his high school yearbook to Mrs. Alice, and explain to her that Stan has died. *She'll remember him.* I looked through each page with Mrs. Alice. She pointed to Sir and said, *Oh, doesn't he look dull!* It was true. The eye that Sir had poked out with a stick when he was a little boy always looked a bit off. We talked about Stan.

Somehow it had come back. Because that's what it does. The cancer. It doesn't care where or how it started, and it doesn't care where or how it's going wherever it's going, but it knows it will get there. The colon, the lungs, the skin, the blood, etcetera, etcetera. It will get there.

Mrs. Alice, I have some sad news to share with you. There was a very long pause. *Mrs. Alice, Sir's been sick, and he had to go back into the hospital again ... Well, let's go visit him ... Well, that's the thing, we can't ... Well, did he die? ...* I do not know how Mrs. Alice knew this, and it felt like my mouth was now somehow broken. *Yes ... Sir has died?! My Sir has died? My Sir? My Sir? Has died? Died? Dead? ...* In this exact second, I knew that Mrs. Alice knew this, but I felt like I was watching this scene from outside of my body, and it just continued to unfold in these elongated seconds that I was no longer directly a part of anymore. *Yes.* But then in less than a minute, it had gone entirely. I had never seen anyone take on such concentrated grief and then, in the same moment, lose it. I searched the grass until I found a tiny divot, and I stared at it until I stopped crying. Then I paused like this: one, two, three, four. I looked at Mrs. Alice. I looked at the divot again.

A few months before this, Sir was on an all-liquid diet in the hospital. Actually, it was worse than liquid only; it was clear liquid only, which basically means water and watered-down apple juice. I was standing at the foot of his bed with Danielle when he said to her, *I know you can get me a cup of coffee*. We all knew he was right because she's from New York, and they don't mess around there. She left for no more than a couple minutes and also returned with a Snickers bar for Sir. He inhaled it. We didn't tell the nurse why his blood sugar went up.

That was the day I drove Mrs. Alice home from visiting Sir. The car ride went like this: I drove Mrs. Alice's car slowly and cautiously. I looked at her as she searched through her purse in the passenger seat. I asked, *What are you looking for? ... Well, my keys, dear. I can't find them! How will we get in the house?! ... It's okay, I have them here with your car keys in the ignition ... Oh my dear, of course, thank you ...* There was a pause of about three blocks through the North Tacoma neighborhoods. I purposefully took the scenic route, not the freeway. Mrs. Alice began to look in her purse again. I asked, *What are you looking for? ... My house keys! I can't find my keys! ... It's okay, Grandma, I have them ... Oh my dear, thank you, of course ...* I went a few more blocks. There was a stop sign. I looked at Mrs. Alice, and she looked at me. I could see she had a sudden realization and started scavenging through her purse. I said, *Mrs. Alice, I have your house key ... Oh! How did you know, dear? ... It's okay, I have it ...* We repeated this many more times — a dozen more at least. That twenty-minute drive seemed to last for days. This scene repeated and repeated, even after turning down her little street, even in her driveway; it repeated. I got out of the car and helped her out, and we walked up the little sidewalk to the front door. Mrs. Alice searched for her keys the entire time. I reassured her that I had them; she thanked me many times.

We went inside. I sat her in Sir's comfy chair, and we talked about the birds in the trees outside. I made up stories and told her of exotic birds I'd seen. None of it was true, but she enjoyed it, so I didn't stop. This felt like fiction being realized, a performance of sorts. It was like a scene from a play, but she didn't know this was all a performance, or maybe she did, but that didn't seem to matter. What mattered is that it was needed, so where does that truth fit in? At this point, I don't so much care anymore. I stayed until she got tired and was ready for bed.

A few months after this, Danielle and I went to Lilly Dale. We went there for the ghosts, of course. We went there because Jess said that this is where you go to find your ghosts again. And I found Sir in the form of a woman. I sat on her couch and patted her cat. She rolled her saliva and started interlacing her fingers so that her knuckles rubbed each time she went back and forth, open and closed with the interlacing. She rubbed her knuckles as if she had chapped arthritic knobs even though she didn't. She told me that since her colon's been shortened, she has to shit all of the time now. *You see, there's less distance for it to travel.* I laughed a little, uncomfortably. She rolled her saliva again. She made that little whistling sound with her teeth: the sound when you suck in, and you think no one can hear this but you. I could hear this. I kept watching her; my back was a chilled ribbon. She leaned forward and complained about how her feet hurt. I asked, *How long have they been hurting you? . . . What do you mean, how long? For as long as I've had feet. That's how long.* There was a pause. Then she said, *You need some money for your trip?* I said, *No, I'm fine . . . Well, good. You know I haven't got any anyway. Ask your mother. She has my money.* There were more things that Sir's ghost-self said. There were things I'd never repeat. Things about babies, about mothers, and about being both of these things. I asked about Mrs. Alice. *Where does she go when her mind disappears?* I could hardly ask this out loud . . . *It's okay, I'm with her in these empty places. We take walks together in her mind.* I started to cry. *It's okay, we just go for walks.* I recorded this woman rolling Sir's saliva, and I listen to the tape when I can't sleep at night. I recorded the whistling and all of these words, too.

When I left her living room, I walked down the street to the lake and put my hands in the water. A sheet of static ran up my back and across the top of my head. My hair went up.

After Sir died, I met with a psychic friend named Lou, and he said that the next time Sir would visit, he would come through an old Grandfather clock. I told Lou I didn't have a clock like this, and in fact, I didn't even have any sort of clock, and he said that was okay. Sir would find his way. I went home to my parent's home, and I walked around from room to room to room. I thought of Sir. I don't know why exactly, but I thought of him, and things seemed to make sense. Then I came to his old clock: the one that used to sit atop the piano; the one you'd have to wind with a key, but ever since Sir died, no one wound it anymore. I looked at it for some time, and then I walked away.

Later that night, my father said that he had recently heard the clock chiming. He said he'd heard it chiming even after he stopped winding it for some time now, and it wasn't chiming upon the hour as it should. I told him about Lou's vision. He explained how the train could have shaken it into chiming. The train does this: it shakes the whole house. *Sure. Sure,* I said.

Just before this, my mother saw Sir in Turkey. She was in a busy outdoor market. He came there as a human mirage and then was gone. And then all her breathing was a stutter. Can I write this here? This is not my story to tell. This is my mother's.

There was a time towards the end that Sir learned how to email. The first email I got from him read, *how are things in denver any snow?* Except that this was all one word. I'd write back elaborate messages, but then I learned that this was too overwhelming. A couple sentences were best.

Sir was quick to learn, and he'd check his email every 20 minutes or so: before and after lunch, and before and after dinner. And just about anytime. Soon enough I got emails that included spaces between the words: *Just thinking about you. Did I spell your name forewords? Say hello to Danielle for me.*

The last email I sent to Sir went like this: *If you're reading this right now, you must be feeling better! You know, you gave us all a real scare there, and you've been doing so well, too. Take your walks again this spring! I love you, Sir.*

Sir never read this.

Yesterday when my mother left Mrs. Alice, she laid her down for a nap, and gave her a little kiss. Mrs. Alice whispered to her, *I'm so glad that we found one another.* This much of a sentence is rare now. She essentially has no more sentences. My mother whispered back, *So am I; so am I.* But then there was more, *Look dear, look. There's a little tear at the corner of my eye, and it won't come out. . . . Oh mom, there is. I'll kiss it out.* There was a short pause. And then my mother said, *Good night, Mom.* And Mrs. Alice replied, *Good night, Mom.* There was a little laugh. *I'm not your mom. . . . No, you're not . . . Who am I? . . . Oh, no, you're not my mom. . . . You're my mom.*

My mother and I were standing in the lobby of the movie theater at the mall. We both started to cry a little. A man came up to us asking for bus fare. We looked at him like he wasn't speaking in sentences because he wasn't. Or we weren't. Or somehow the language was just confused.

I've never witnessed the death of a human before — that exact moment of migration. Last year at this time, Chelsea dog and I watched a mouse die. We came across it in Edna's field between the barn and the house. It was struggling, and Chelsea wanted to play with it. I held her back. It was twitching, rolling on its back. I didn't know what to do, so I just kept holding onto Chelsea, and she started barking. The mouse stopped moving a minute or two later. That was when Chelsea really went wild. I couldn't hold her anymore. She kept jumping in the air, barking up, up, and then over and up, away from the mouse's body. Then everything was still. The air, the dog, the mouse. We took the mouse to the creek and laid it there to rest.

Later I took a ghost tour at the hotel from *The Shining*. The guide said that animals and children see a level of light that adults can't see anymore. *This is where the spirits exist*, he said to us in the hallway in front of the room where Stephen King used to write. Everyone nodded. The children in the tour group ran up and down the hallway.

The longest relationship I've ever been in is the one that ended on Saturday. It'd been nearly six years, which is little less that nine percent of seventy.

Mrs. Alice, how long is seventy years? ... You don't want to know ... But I do.

I do not know what it is like to know someone for seventy years, but then to not actually know this. To not know that they have died. To not know that you don't get to know them anymore. I think it means that Mrs. Alice gets to keep knowing Sir. And I think that this must be grief in its most idyllic form. Or at least, I like to hope it is.

I haven't yet read the page about how to lament. Please, tell me.

The first time I was ever called Sir, I was eleven years old. Maybe I was twelve, but that's not important. I held the door open for Santa at the post office, and he thanked me, *Sir.*

I went home, shut myself in my room, looked in the mirror, and said to myself, *I am not a sir!*

Someone said, *rain is confession weather*. Who said that? Why? What did it feel like to move from California to Washington? *Mrs. Alice, where do you live? ... Colorado.* This was one question the dementia facility asked her to see if she qualified. They made a check mark.

I cannot always remember what it is like to stand next to another human anymore. By this I mean, what it is like to stand next to every room in their body.

I like to drink my earl grey tea just after I've brushed my teeth because it tastes extra fresh like this — like it's from the produce department or something. No one knows this anymore. Every year, I Photoshop my college ID to keep it current, and then I go to the opera where it makes my body feel both foreign and local at the same, and I like this contradiction. It's the same way I feel when I write about how the word *and* is different from the word *human.* And I think that if everyone could just be a little more *and*, we'd all be a lot better off.

I want to know these things about another human.

The house that I'm now living in has a television, which is the first time I've lived with a television since I was in high school and lived at home. I've now learned from Oprah what forgiveness means. She said that to forgive someone means that you've realized you do not wish you were any different than you are right now. This does not mean that you must love what is to be forgiven... Or it went something like this... *There were no colors. This never happened.*

I understand now that this is what happens when a *human* tries to become an *and:* the language won't let us.

If it's actually true that *all poets teach how to lament*, then why is it that I don't know how, yet?

What is the difference between grief and lamentation?

Please, won't someone just tell me already?

After my thirteenth birthday, I was having nightmares every night, so I would go downstairs to sleep on the couch because it seemed safest there. I heard the phone ring at 6:00 a.m. a few days after the New Year, but the only part I remember is my mother saying words like *oh* and then *oh*. This is how language fails us when it's the only thing that's actually needed — being on the phone and such.

This was the first time I learned that early morning phone calls are not very good. Now when it rings early, I think, *prepare yourself, the language might fail.*

I'm writing these stories in reverse now because I can't remember how to emit time anymore. I wanted to curse Sir. *Don't you know she's got no memory!?* But the one from sixty years ago is like a glass of water only even more clear: it doesn't even have that distorted part at the lip: the part where you can't tell how tall something is. The problem is is that her sentences have to exist right now. This is what the limit of her body is.

Sometimes I think about what it is like to live in Colorado now for the first time in three generations, and I wonder if the memory of the body might be genetic.

Mrs. Alice, what are the limits of the body?

This is… This is…

And then that was it. It was like she had forgotten how to make a sentence anymore. This is *what*? *What* is this? Or was it, This is, *period.* I'm so afraid of this. I want to make these sentences. And I want to make them sixty years from now, too.

I work most days as a book designer, and two nights ago, I was working on a text about phenomena when I noticed that something strange was happening with the letters. I zoomed in and in and more and again. I saw each letter up closely, and I saw that they were breathing — literally and slowly. Maybe you don't believe me, but I saw this vividly. It was like the letters were made of tiny humans lying on their backs with their arms crossed over their chests. They looked something like miniature living corpses on their deathbeds. It seemed that they might be suffocating one another — being so closely piled. So I gave space around each letter and word and line and margin, and then I zoomed back in and in and more closely still, and again, and they had stopped. Entirely. There was no more breathing — not even slowly, not even a little.

From inside of my dream, Sir asked me if I was dreaming. I said, *I don't think so.* He said, *you know, this is where the word goes when it's ready to die. It goes inside the book, and it holds itself here.*

The next morning, I got a phone call that the author had died.

Dear Sir,

Can I still write you little letters even though you're dead now?

Please say *yes.*

Dear Sir,

I know you're here again — moving that tiny iron and placing it next to its tiny trivet. That was a good one. Like how you used to turn my baseball trophies ten degrees to see if I'd notice. I noticed.

Dear Sir,

I arrived in Washington earlier today. It's not even been 24 hours since your death, and now I'm washing the dishes you left in your sink. Your cereal bowl, your coffee mug with the blue bottom and the stained white top, the spoon with the spongy grip because of your arthritis. The scrubber was still wet and sitting on the lip of your sink, and I thought about how I was feeling you here in this dampness. How was your last bowl of cereal? How was your last cup of coffee? Did you enjoy them or was it all just very regular?

Mrs. Alice doesn't even know yet. Sir, what are we supposed to say? I mean I know she won't remember, but really, what do we say to her?

I rolled up your rug, carried out your favorite chair, put your television on the hand-truck, and we donated it all. Even the two new polo shirts with pockets that I got you for Christmas. They were still soft, and I ate the Worthers' candy you left in each pocket. Your alarm clock, side table, large-print books, and laundry basket. We took it all to the Catholic charity house where my friend used to teach English classes to Spanish migrant workers and their children.

I thought about how the last time I was in your room, you asked me to help you button your pants, and I said *no* and then sort of made fun of you. I'm very sorry, Sir. I shouldn't have done that.

Is "I'm sorry" real to a dead person?

Dear Sir,

Yesterday was your memorial. We put your ashes in the bay just beyond the Golden Gate. And we went up Mt. Tam and walked around. I think I was twelve-years-old yesterday. I raced you to the lookout tower, and you said I only won because you'd just stopped training, and you were supposed to take it easy for a while. *Training for what?* I asked, and you said, *Training for the Presidency, of course.* You said this like it made sense, and it did.

We found Mike, or he found us. I'm not quite sure how it all happened. He's here in this city, dressed in a tux and top hat all made of comic strips. He said he sleeps in the trees. I don't know if you want to hear this or not, Sir, but there it is. Here he is.

Dear Sir,

Last month, a woman came up to me in the airport and asked about my thoughts on communing with the dead. I don't know how our conversation got like this so quickly, but I do know that she was very forward. She said that she thought that you and I are spirit twins or something like this. I said, *I don't know anything about that.* She said we'd always be present in one another's lives.

Sir, are you back yet?

Will you be my son?

I hope you like the names we're choosing.

Dear Sir,

When Mrs. Alice and I were sitting outside on Wednesday, I saw you as you went by, whispering, *I'm okay, dear. I'm okay, dear. I'm okay, dear.*

You were tall again, and the cancer was gone; your arthritis — gone. You didn't even have that big knobby thing on your elbow anymore. I'd never seen you like this before — like you actually were okay.

You had a harmonica in your shirt pocket and two books on the tarot in your left hand. As you passed us by, you handed me the Fool card. I had a flash-back to my mother leaving for work in the morning when I was still a little girl, and she would always say to me, *Kiss me like a fool.*

Dear Sir,

I was at your house today helping my mother clean up your yard before we sell it. Your neighbors miss you. The guy on the North side gave us good advice about what to say to Mrs. Alice though. Not for the first time, but just in general, when she asks, *Where's Sir?* And you know she asks about you. He said just say, *Sir couldn't make it today.*

Is that okay with you? It's too depressing to always say that you're dead. She hears everything for the first time, and we just can't say this to her more than once. It's too awful to watch. You know, Sir? I don't mean any disrespect, but I just can't put that grief on her all the time. I mean, she knows; I believe this; she knows.

Dear Sir,

Last night, I heard you calling from the top of the brick silo where the bees are kept. You were shouting, *I'm up here now!* But Sir, what if I don't believe in heaven? I tried to run up the stairs to you, but they kept changing their direction, and then I was running down and sideways toward the sounds of you whistling through your front teeth like how you used to make wind sounds.

Dear Sir,

Yesterday, we spent mother's day with Mrs. Alice. My mother was showing off her new necklace, and Mrs. Alice was concentrating on it so strongly that it was like she was trying to figure out an algebra problem or the meaning of life or something like this entirely beyond the necklace. Mom said, *Well, what do you think of it? Isn't it beautiful?* Mrs. Alice leaned back in her chair and asked, *but where does it begin?*

Yes, *where does it begin?*

It's not such a strange question really. I mean, is it?

Dear Sir,

Last night I was given a handful of your ashes. I put half of you in my garden — mulched you in around the irises whose bulbs Patty dug last spring from your front yard just before we sold your home. I hope you like it here.

I hid your other half, but I can't remember where I put you now. I only told Mrs. Alice, and she can't remember either. I'm very sorry, Sir, but I think I might have lost part of you. I promise, I'll try to re-dream this tonight, but until then, can you be safe in the memory of whiteness?

Dear Sir,

It has been exactly one year since your death. Tonight's the night —
just after midnight. You haven't visited me for a couple of months.
Since just after my birthday. Except for last night when the dog was
sleeping with me, curled at the foot, and her breathing was different
— heavy, like an old man's, like yours when you'd fall asleep in the
living room chair. I'm twenty-seven now, and I'm trying to remember
everything as best as I can. Like that summer when we were playing
basketball, and you were wearing those funny teal shorts with the faded
orange pockets, and Cookie came out in her bathrobe to make fun of
you from the other side of the driveway. I'm putting this here. This isn't
good enough! Is this good enough?

You know, I didn't start this because you died, Sir. That just happened.
It was like you had a terrible stomachache, but you always ached, and
then the doctor said, *it's back*, and you were so afraid you'd suffer, but
then all of a sudden I'm quoting John Wayne on the little card about
your death, and we passed it out to everyone you knew. *Tomorrow comes
into us at midnight very clean. It's perfect when it arrives. It puts itself in our hands,
and it hopes we've learned something from yesterday.* No. No, Sir. I started this
because I'm afraid of not remembering, and then Mrs. Alice said that
the evergreen across the street was looking like, well that it was looking
like something she just couldn't quite remember right then, and then
she couldn't remember what we were talking about anymore, and then
she couldn't remember that she was speaking a sentence at all, and so
she just smiled at me, and I said, *I wish I knew how long 70 years was*, and she
said, *you don't want to know*, and I said, *but I do*. And then next time, Mrs. Alice
said, *don't miss anything*. And I told her I wouldn't. No Sir, This is supposed
to be about the living, and this is supposed to be about remembering
that we are the living.

Dear Sir,

I've just learned of a friend who's died. She had written, *dead person, dead person, will you partake in my persimmon feast?* Sir, let's have a hard-candy feast and go for a walk.

I hate this death. Makes me feel like we're all just running out of time, and what exactly am I doing just sitting here on this airplane like really, is one side more urgent than the other? Is it? Please, Sir, tell me I'll live to be infinity because I couldn't take it otherwise.

Dear Sir,

If I died today, then everyone will know that I never took a shower this morning. The time is now 2:17 pm in the great state of Colorado, I'm still in my pajamas, and I don't plan on changing this later today either. Today. Today. Today, today, today. Does anyone ever get to know that they're going to die today? Sir, did you know when the most intimate moment of your life was here? Was that why you waited for my mother to leave the room and then for the woman from Hospice to leave the room, and then the clock went past midnight, and you were alone in your room? *Tomorrow comes into us at midnight very clean. It's perfect when it arrives...* Was it perfect for you, Sir?

At least it was no longer today.

Dear Sir,

Do you believe in ghosts? I never did, but I'm not really sure anymore. I moved back to Boulder almost two months ago now, and I'm living in Anne's house on 45th Street. It's temporary, you know. I'm just trying to get things back in order in my mind, and this is a good place to be for the winter. But there's so many ghosts here, and I don't mean just you. They go up and down the stairs, and run the water, and chime things. It gets pretty strange here when it's late, and I think, I'm taking on Anne's sleeping schedule, and I don't go to bed before four in the morning or more because there's just too much going on in this house. I mean, they're chiming things all night long, Sir. Can you hear them?

Dear Sir,

Do you think it's possible for the dead to visit through the living? In September, I saw Akilah on the subway when I was back in New York for a couple few days. It was late, and we were on our way home. Rachel and Nic were sitting across from me, and Akilah was on my left. I mean, of course it wasn't really her, but I kept looking at her eyes, and she would close them, and then open them and look at me, and close them again, and then open them and look at Rachel, and then repeat. I didn't say anything to anyone.

Two weeks later, I saw Bernie in Kansas City. She said her name was Bee, and she was 93 years old — a retired English teacher who likes to write poems. She invited me back to her house to play Scrabble, but I said I couldn't go. No, I couldn't go because her voice sounded too much like Bernie's, and by that, I don't actually mean *sounded like*, I mean, her voice *was* Bernie's. Everything she said was the same, and I kept flashing back to when I turned thirteen, and she lived in my parents bedroom, and everyday when I'd come home from basketball practice, she was rocking in her chair in the living room and sipping chicken broth from a coffee cup. I was afraid that Bee would offer me chicken broth that evening, and I would have no response that was good enough — being a vegetarian now and all. So instead we sat on that bench in Kansas City, and we talked about how language is responsible for everything we'll ever know, and that that's a pretty big responsibility for one thing to have. She took my picture in front of the antique taxidermied pheasants and peacocks, and I left.

Dear Sir,

Do you think that excessively using the word *and* makes a person sound manic? Brian said this in a writing workshop last year, but I love this word. I'm getting *and* tattooed on my wrist in 6 hours and 14 minutes. Is that stupid? Is that hypocritical — being a human and all? I want it forever. I want the *and* life, and I'm serious about that. *And* never knows any limits to its body; *and* knows no limits because it's incapable of ever even thinking about *no*. That's just not possible. I have to write the human narrative, but can only theorize about *and* because that's not my reality. What a sham. *And* has it made, Sir; it gets to be everything; it's better than god or the world or love or anything (these things are just too human). I can only describe it by saying, *and*. And in my next life, I want to be an *and*, not a *human*. I just want to live amongst the other *ands*.

Dear Sir,

I've stopped trusting other humans. I do like talking to Mrs. Alice though because she can't hold any of my sentences once they're complete. I write things in this notebook like it's the only partner I'll ever have, but if anyone ever read these thoughts, I'd be mortified. I'm obsessively aware of it's location, which is always within my reach, and then when the notebook is full, I duct tape it closed. I admit, I'm getting paranoid about this, but I have to protect my body.

Dear Sir,

My favorite thing about the word *human* is that it's genderless. Even *person* sometimes only means men. How did that happen?

What does it mean to be a human alongside another human? That was the original question of this project. Sir, I wanted to interview you and Mrs. Alice and just ask this question repetitively (*There is no such thing as repetition. Only insistence.*), but now you're dead, and Mrs. Alice can't carry a conversation.

How long is 70 years? I don't know any human that has lived alongside another human for this long because they're all either dead now, or they just couldn't make it.

I feel like a hypocrite writing this project because Danielle said she wanted to be on her own now. I mean, what the hell do I know about being a human alongside another human? Clearly not very much. It was a Saturday, and I was making tea, and I felt like my knees had been removed and then reinserted backwards. I never drank that cup of tea.

I don't know what to do in this exact minute. I walk around the house; I brush my teeth, make tea. I sit here, and then I sit here. I just want to wake up along side another human again, and we could just be lazy all day together. But being lazy by myself is just plain lonely.

Sorry, I know this letter is pathetic, Sir. I'll try again tomorrow.

Dear Sir,

What does a dream look like when you're dead? I mean, does the question *what's next,* become invalid? That seems like such a static place to be. I don't ever want to make this question invalid. Please help me.

Sir, there's ghosts in this house, and they live on the stairs.

Dear Sir,

Write me a manual. I'll believe you; I will. Make it full of blank pages, and I'll only believe myself.

Yesterday when I put on your wool plaid jacket, Bobbie said to me, *Oh my dear, how lucky.* I said, *what do you mean?* She said, *every time you put on Sir's jacket, you get to wrap yourself in stories... Yes, this is my favorite part about getting dressed.* And so I do this everyday. So much so that I schedule when to go to the dry cleaners a few weeks ahead of time so that I'm not too lonely for those days. This is a form of preparation.

Dear Sir,

I'm becoming obsessive with numbers. No, not numbers, but one number: 217, the number of the house I grew-up in. I see it everywhere. Right now I'm sitting at gate 217 waiting for a bus to take me out of New York City. We're due to arrive in Providence at 2:17 pm. I like to think that when I see this number, I know I'm making the right decision. Don't tell me this is silly. Last week, I met this woman, and her birthday is February seventeenth. I want to befriend her simply because of this, but I won't tell her this because that'd be weird.

Dear Sir,

My mother just gave me a pile of all the letters I've ever written to you and Mrs. Alice. Everything is there: the envelopes, photos, newspaper clippings, stickers, drawings, and so much language. I haven't read them all. I've barely begun. There's a valentine to you from when I'm nine, and it's written in a spiral heart shape. There's a ransom note I collaged chastising you for not writing me back, yet. There's a scribble from when I'm three. There's a letter about how terrible the ninth-grade dance was — how Matt left me right when we got there because he really wanted to go with Angela to begin with, but he still took photos with me in front of the glitter balloons, and then there's that awful photo. There's clippings of every article I wrote for the school paper. There's a letter on a doily, one on a napkin, one on a postcard with a hot air balloon, and a postcard with the Northern Lights, and a postcard with a snowman, and a postcard with the New York City skyline, and a postcard with the Flat Irons, and a postcard from Japan, and a postcard with a guide dog for the blind who's wearing a Santa hat. There's ninety-six of these letters, Sir. Mrs. Alice kept them all, and I had no idea. She kept them in *the basket*, as she called it, but I was never allowed to look in there.

Dear Sir,

Mrs. Alice has lost more of her language. She just repeats words that I've said. Like a little mimicker, like a kid learning these syllables for the first time. She can't answer a question anymore. A question is not a viable thing.

Mrs, Alice, What are the limits of the body?

A quiet stare.

I show her photos from trips I've taken, and I make up elaborate stories full of characters I haven't yet met. I can tell that she likes this. We sit together, and I act out lines from the play I've been working on. I like to say my lines in a Shakespearian voice: *So scene of looming figure.* I show her the choreography that goes along with this part and pantomime that I'm a prisoner picking weeds along the side of the road. She laughs at me when that's not the funny part, and I like this.

Dear Sir,

I understand now that there is a difference between being social and being in the company of another. Do you think Mrs. Alice is lonely? Are *you* lonely, Sir? Why would Mrs. Alice say that thing to me about seventy years?

How long is seventy years? ... You don't want to know.

I do want to know. Seventy years from now, I'll be ninety-eight, and I expect to be alive then. Yes, I expect this of myself.

Dear Sir,

Last night Mrs. Alice told me when she's going to die. I know this was only as a dream, but what do I do? Lilly was dancing around her — twirling, twirling — and then my mother asked, *What are you thinking about, Mom? ... Well, Sir is here ... Oh? ... Yes, he says he'll give me his hand again on Friday. He'll help me come to him on Friday because he misses me, and he's going to help me. On Friday. Friday. He's going to help me on Friday.*

Sir, is this true? Oh, please help me to stop thinking about this. Today is Wednesday. Not yet. No, not yet, Sir. I'm not ready.

Please Sir, don't visit me in the night like this again. I do not want to carry this language. Do not give it to me anymore.

Dear Sir,

I've just spent five days in a room that looked like the inside of a purse. This is what Serena said the second when we walked in, and she was right. During the days, I sold books like a used-car salesman, and then we'd go dancing until light time. We'd come back to our purse room, pass out for a few hours, hop ourselves up on vitamin C, and then return to selling the language. No one recognized this as unnatural.

But then I stole a box of wine. This was the guilty part. Somehow we had earned this cheap wine though. Yes, we earned this. Krystal said so, and I believed her.

This was when things were measured in Ferris wheels and spherical mirrors that reflected the city. This was when I said, *Take me, I want this language!* I want to say this right now, but this would be fiction.

Dear Sir,

I realize now that all the world's about showing up. That's it: just showing up. When I think about killing myself, I wonder if I already have. I can't decide if I feel like a crazy person all of the time or just most of the time. The problem is that I may never know. *There's a night when you don't say words. Do you know that? No. I don't know it.* I yell at myself, *show up, show up!* I am making this my mantra. *I am calling to my future self again.* Do I know this? Yes, I know this.

Dear Sir,

Where are you in your migration? Is there a language there, and can you read my letters? You've stopped responding. Everyday I wear your wool plaid jacket, and I think about the stories I'm wrapping myself in. I get to do this. I get to wrap myself in your stories every day, and this is my favorite part about getting dressed. I mean, this is *why* I get dressed some days. I enter the world as a human like this. Like a sir, Sir. My hips hold each jacket pocket, and I place my hands here. I mean, you'd place your hands here, right? I want to wrap myself like this for as long as my human life will allow.

Put your hand in here: a damp translucence, a natural saturation.

Dear Sir,

I can't remember how to go into the place where the words exist as sentences. How do you say noun then verb and have it sound right? I just want it all to sound right again. Noun verb. Noun verb. Noun verb. No, no. That's backwards, isn't it? How's it go again? Is it verb noun now in this language? Yes, yes, I think that's right. Sir, please hear me. I am calling to you from this place of *and*. I can't find the nouns and verbs.

Dear Sir,

I want to tell you that I'm wrapping my bodies with your stories.

Dear Sir,

I've been having a problem with the onwards part. I'm in a stagnant space about Danielle, and all I want is to feel the greatest good again. You know what I mean? Sir, tell me about the time when you and Mrs. Alice were not together. Tell me these stories. Who was he — that boy named Buddy? What happened? Start from the beginning. Everything I do not know.

Dear Sir,

What does it mean to want to hope for something when that something is human? Does that mean I'm naïve? I am not convinced. I only want to hear what is true, so tell it to me. I promise I'll believe you.

Today my horoscope said that impulsiveness isn't good for sustained growth. I don't want to believe this. Where is the point where impulse crosses thoughtfulness? There must be a point; there must be an alleyway. I want to go to this crossroad and stay there for a while. Please Sir, *take my hand, lead me on.*

Dear Sir,

I want to walk with you through these fields again. I want to eat all your Worthers', and snake the frogs, and bring them into our tree house family; and I want to tell you about how this place is now. How it's just full of the dead and the demented. And then you would say, *Compared to what?* And I want to watch you stare at me until I laugh. And then you would say, *Here: take this hammer, and go pound back down those nails over there.*

Dear Sir,

When do I get to be *and* now?

All I want to do is say, *I and you* in the way where *and* is a verb, like I *do* this. I *love* you. I *and* you. Do you understand what I am saying now?

How do I account for the space between paragraphs? Sir, this question haunts me, Sir. Please, make it stop. I want the spaces to stop being so fond of the gaps. I am writing to you from here: from the place where language doesn't sound like a sentence anymore because it has forgotten its breath.

Does this just mean that I am still arriving? Andrea says *their lungs helped them to arrive.* Sir, why won't my lungs help me like this? I move them, I do — like this and sometimes a little bit more like this, but they forget.

Dear Sir,

What does a shadow look like when you're dead? Is a penumbra sort of like the two words *Mark Twain* — the place where the safe water begins, but in a shadowy form, not in a watery form? Sir, I am making us a language! Come and meet me here. I am extending to you these middle waters and these middle shadows. This is a held place. Believe me, I have been here for a while now, and I still want to be *and* now.

Dear Sir,

I am trying on narrations, and this is what it feels like: a pocket of red string.

Look, look, look, it's like this: I can either see the humans right now or I can see the words, so the humans are going to get a bit blurry. I want the words. That's all that I want. This is a want that has all together forgotten what to do with wanting.

Dear Sir,

I am afraid to say, *I love you* — a collection of simple sounds. I know this is the softest room in the body, but the navigation is so —. This is what it means to swim in a vivisection, and I like swimming; I do, but I need the tide to be more clear. By this, I mean my thoughts: I need them to just stay a little longer. Please Sir, just stay a little bit longer now. Come with me! It's time to walk.

Please, help me to hallucinate a clear tide.

Dear Sir,

Were you here again last night? I'm a little bit confused. I heard you in the echoes when you said, *Watch out! This is your body.* But then I couldn't find you, and I looked; I really did.

But then I took that bit of blow from that boy who told me his name was Peter Valentine, and I wanted to believe him.

Sir, I am evacuating all of my bodies.

Dear Sir,

Last night I watched Dan walked out the window of his high-rise apartment. I followed him. *Someone else* watched us do this.

Then I awoke to Danielle calling me, and when I answered she said, *Thank god you're alive!*

Later, Rachel asked if anyone else dreamt about the apocalypse last night. Yes. Sir, *if living had to be about the body, who made it so?*

Dear Sir,

What time is it? A damp translation. A row boat. *A sack of a baby.*

This is gone though, Sir. *Of ever imagining that.*

Don't you get it now, Sir?! *Or ever having wanted that.*

Listen to me, Sir. I know what I'm talking about! *Or known it. From someone.*

Sir, are you *someone*? No, you're just a ghost. A spook. A haunt and a specter. You're a shadow now, Sir, and you can't even visit these colors anymore.

What is it like? Is it like skittering? Please, take my hand. Tell me it is.

Dear Sir,

I'm twenty-eight now, and these bodies are moving quickly, no? What were you doing when you turned twenty-eight years old? It was 1953, and my mother was eight months away from being born. Did you know this?

I'm getting back to being a human again, and I guess this is what it feels like: I had forgotten how cold it can get in bed at night when you're only one human.

Oh Sir, I just wish you were here again to say *human* how you always would — how you'd keep the *h* silent. And I would say, *uman is not a word, Sir.* And you would say, *Well, of course it is. I just said it.*

Who we are when we are not love has always caused us shame.

A KILAH OLIVER

ACKNOWLEGMENTS

I am indebted to my grandparents, Ray and Lilah Hook, who have inspired the characters of Sir and Mrs. Alice. I hope I didn't miss anything.

Thank you to Brenda Iijima for the support and encouragement that has made this project possible from its earliest pages. Thank you to Anne Waldman, Rachel Levitsky, Andrea Rexilius, Danielle Vogel, Serena Chopra, and Lisa Vallejos for the conversations about what it means to be a human alongside another human. Thank you to my family for being these humans.

The majority of this manuscript was written during the days before and after three annual retreats with the Belladonna* Collaborative at the Millay Colony.

And with grace in our onwards, thank you to Selah Saterstrom. You are the personification of *and*.

NOTES

Page 35: *"Rain is confession weather."* is a line from "Speech Bubbles" on the *Elephant Eyelash* album by Why? (Anticon Records, 2005).

Page 37: *"There were no colors. This never happened."* was redacted from *Essay on Ash*, a film by Ed Bowes, script by Laird Hunt (Walsung Compang).

Page 38: *"All poets teach how to lament."* is a line from Akilah Oliver.

Pages 40 & 65: *"What are the limits of the body?"* is a question that Akilah Oliver asked in a writing workshop during the 2007 Summer Writing Program at Naropa University.

Page 41: "Text about phenomena" is a reference to the book *How Phenomena Appear to Unfold* by Leslie Scalapino (Litmus Press, 2011).

Page 45: *"Is 'I'm sorry' real to a dead person?"* is a line from the poem "In Aporia" in the book *A Toast in the House of Friends* by Akilah Oliver (Coffee House Press, 2009).

Pages 53 & 55: *"Tomorrow comes into us at midnight very clean. It's perfect when it arrives. It puts itself in our hands, and it hopes we've learned something from yesterday."* is a John Wayne quotation from a 1971 *Playboy* interview.

Page 54, *"Dead person, dead person, will you partake in my persimmon feast?"* is a line from the poem "In Aporia" in the book *A Toast in the House of Friends* by Akilah Oliver (Coffee House Press, 2009).

Page 60: *"There is no such thing as repetition. Only insistence."* is by Gertrude Stein.

Page 65: *"So scene of looming figure"* is a line from "Sweet, A Play" in the book *How Phenomena Appear to Unfold* by Leslie Scalapino (Litmus Press, 2011).

Page 69: *"There's a night when you don't say words. Do you know that? No. I don't know it... I am calling to my future self again."* are lines from Alice Notely's reading at Naropa University on Febrary 24, 2012.

Page 74: *"Take my hand, lead me on."* is a line from the poem "she said, talk to grandmother in cycles: cycle 3" in the book *the she said dialogues: flesh memory* by Akilah Oliver (Smokeproof Press and Erudite Fangs, 1999).

Page 75: *"Compared to what?"* is a line from *Marcel the Shell with Shoes On*, directed by Dean Fleischer-Camp.

Page 76: *"How do I account for the space between paragraphs?"* was redacted from Danielle Vogel's essay "The Threshing Floor: Akilah Oliver & A Potential Hermeneutics of Grief"

Page 76: *"Their lungs helped them to arrive."* is a line from the poem "First Residence: Desire" in the book *Half of What they Carried Flew Away* by Andrea Rexilius (Letter Machine Editions, 2012).

Page 77: The reference to "penumbra" was inspired by the chapbook *Penumbra* by Serena Chopra (Flying Guillotine Press, 2012).

Page 81: *"If living had to be about the body, who made it so?"* is a line from Alice Notely's book *Songs and Stories of the Ghouls* (Wesleyan, 2011).

Page 82: *"A sack of a baby... Of ever imagining that... Or ever having wanted that...Or known it. From someone."* are lines from "Sweet, A Play" in the book *How Phenomena Appear to Unfold* by Leslie Scalapino (Litmus Press, 2011).

HR HEGNAUER

HR Hegnauer is a book designer and website designer specializing in working with independent publishers as well as individual artists and writers. She is a member of the feminist publishing collaborative Belladonna*, and she's part of the poets' theater group GASP: Girls Assembling Something Perpetual. HR received her MFA in Writing & Poetics from Naropa University, where she has also taught in the Summer Writing Program. *Sir* is her first book.